Girl Stop Running

Girl stop running and accept You...
stand and fight the good fight to live
by the promises of God.
Fight for your faith!
Fight to be You!
Fight to live free!

1 Timothy 6:12 MSG

November Media Publishing Copyright © 2023

Myrtice Carter All rights reserved.

No part of this publication may be reproduced, distributed, or transmitted in any form or by any means, including photocopying, recording, or other electronic or mechanical methods, without the prior written permission of the publisher, except in the case of brief quotations embodied in critical reviews and certain other noncommercial uses permitted by copyright law.

For permission requests, write to the author, addressed "Attention: Myrtice Carter," at the email address below.
Myrtice@myrticecarter.com

Ordering Information:
Special discounts are available on quantity purchases by corporations, associations, and others. For details, contact the author at the email address above.

Printed in the United States of America
ISBN: 978-1-0881-6728-1

Scripture references: KJV Bible, English Standard Version,
New International Version, and Gods Word
Versions First Edition: May 2023
10 9 8 7 6 5 4 3 2 1

Dedication

This book is for those who have been affected by rejection, who have always felt like a responsible child (who grew up too fast), overcomers, and go-getters, as well as:

- ✦ Anyone struggling with a hustle.
- ✦ Career females who struggle with confidence, unhealthy relationships, and lifestyle balance.
- ✦ Females seeking support on maintaining boundaries and positivity.
- ✦ All those that have experienced or are still experiencing brokenness due to being raised in a single family, co-dependency, or childhood trauma.
- ✦ Those just ready for IT to be over.
- ✦ Those that are ready to evolve!

Letter from the author

The time has come for me to birth this book. Oh, what a journey it has been to get to this point! It's been full of loving, living, and exploring adulthood and it hasn't been all good, but definitely not all bad. As I reflect on my 37 years on this earth, I am also confident that my story, journey, life— whichever one you want to call it— will help someone, and that will be my greatest blessing. So now I would like to share with you what I wish I had heard early in my journey to becoming this new version of me. While on this journey, I did many things to grow beyond my IT, where I was stuck, felt uneasy, lacked the right mindset, or just felt totally unconfident. After years of feeling this way, I decided it was time to do some work and move past the *ish*. Now it's called *self-care* work, but I called it "Me Phi Me" work back in 2015, lol. Was it easy? No. Was it worth it? Yes, I felt as though I went back to school for a degree in Life 101, lol. I grew, and so did my life.

Often, our IT has a name, but we fail to call it for what it is or give it a proper title. I did it too. Sometimes IT is fear, shame, people pleasing, being overworked and underpaid, family issues, relationship problems, weight gain, grief, emotional eating, bad habits, just nonstop chaos, etc. On the other hand, it might be an action we need to take to release us from those listed in the above sentence. It was not until a counseling session in 2022 that I was able to start labeling my IT. So, in this book, I will help you label and release your IT. I will describe a few of the ITs many of us face and have faced and the tools used to persevere through them. With each chapter, I will provide you with a definition of the action word and a scripture to aid in your understanding.

As you begin reading, I really want you to allow yourself to be open to messages, feelings, and actions that might surface and that you might need to embrace. You may consider journaling your thoughts as you go (which I highly encourage) or using breathing techniques when negative emotions or anxiety arise. You should also accept that there is nothing wrong with crying, praying and pausing, and coming back to reading when you're ready to be open. Please, please, don't fall into the information overload. Be gentle with yourself! Rome wasn't built in a day, as they say, lol. Either way, continue until you reach the end of the book. I allowed myself to push through to write it and read it multiple times and so you can push too! Push beyond the unhealthy boundaries set by others, and maybe even you, then go grow. It's bamboo season!

Love, Myrtice Carter

Introduction

Girl Stop Running is intended to help you grow mentally and spiritually, as this will allow you to make the best decisions for your life without feeling guilty. As Sarah Jakes Roberts says, *I'm intentionally preparing to loosen the chains from someone's life by writing this book!*

This book might be focused on ladies but caters to everyone who has faced situations that made them feel unseen. It will also help you improve your identity and erase any labels society may have thrown at you. It is time to grow beyond both, unseen and mislabeled versions of you and live life on God's and your terms. It has taken me over seven years to write my first book, which started in 2016 as a journal, because of many unforeseen challenges. Then, in 2021, I was challenged to write a book by the end of the year. Still no luck. Yet, with great determination, I vowed to do it in 2022, and within the last three months of the year, I completed a draft of this book. Now I am excited to share my growth journey with you!

Foreword

Girl, Stop Running...wow!

What an appropriate title and a timely book. I'm super proud of Myrtice Carter. I can actually say *I knew her when.* I love seeing her drive, growth, and determination to take whatever life throws her way and rise to the occasion. Myrtice is the true definition of "resilience" and "perseverance," and her story is far from over. If you need a dose of motivation and a friendly reminder of who you are, look no further. Her life is a brilliant testimony for all of us to learn from while we celebrate her gift. In true Myrtice fashion, she guides us on a journey (page by page) to own our IT. This book is jam-packed with wisdom, knowledge, and moments of reflection to help you look inward and upward.

Thank you, Myrtice, for your hunger to grow and take us with you.

Signed, a girl no longer on the run!
Tasha M. Scott, owner of Maximized Growth, LLC

1. Rejection

Rejection: the action of rejecting or the state of being rejected. (Merriam-Webster Dictionary)
For the Lord will not cast off His people, nor will He forsake His inheritance. (NKJV Psalms 94:14)

Shout out to all the people, places, and things that rejected me, caused fear, and dehumanized me! They drove me to face the fake ME I was portraying and to find the true ME!

REJECTION is hard, as no one wants to feel left out, unseen, or made to feel invaluable. It hurts to the core of our souls at times, depending on the source of the rejection. The closer the person was to you that inflicted the hurt, the sharper the pain. It hurts like stomping a pinky toe, thus sending an eerie feeling of pain up the body and an "Oh sh**" out of your mouth. Some of us have experienced this rejection from childhood up until adulthood. If you're reading this and have not, you are fortunate, but it is inevitable that you will feel rejection at some point, and I hope that you will remember this book when you do.

The good thing I have learned is that rejection is only temporary, as there will be something that comes in and helps remove the sting or source of the pain, and you will receive the desired relief. The key thing is that we have to get to a place where we release it back out the same way it came in. My go-to mantras/scriptures, whichever your choice may be, are "This too shall pass" and "I forgive myself and release anything that does not serve me now." Whatever works for you. I suggest you use the energy from the rejection as fuel to reach another goal or complete another task. Don't waste it on reliving the situation(s). Yeah, you know every part of the story, and the should've, could've, and would've too, but unfortunately, that moment has passed, and new good memories are ready to be made.

I can remember that as a kid, I loved being with my family. I gloried at the idea of being a daddy's girl that went everywhere with him in his fast car (79 Pontiac Firebird Trans Am), and I enjoyed swimming at the lake in the summers with my family. My favorite memories are of Mom taking us on "kids eat free" nights on our infamous pizza hut trips with my cousins. It was always family. But as I got older, reality began to shine through to reveal the unhealthiest parts of my family, and the rejection and abandonment set in. The family I had known my entire life began to fall apart. Divorce meant no more time with Dad and no more trips cause the money wasn't there. Then, we had to move away from our childhood friends to live with Grandma.

It all became different, including lies from family to hide the truth or in their mind prevent damage to my mind. Still, even back then, I felt as if everyone was out to hurt and leave me. It began to shift me to a place of heartlessness. For example, I would project my insecurities onto my brother's relationships with girls because I felt as though they were taking his time away from me. My brother was my first best friend, and he couldn't leave me too. It sucked, and as a preteen, I hated it. Fast forward to college, I began to shift my focus and growth beyond my feelings of "everyone is leaving me" and accepted that it was ok for me to be on my own. Now, I understand that just because things were different, that didn't mean I wasn't loved or couldn't be the person I wanted to be. We have to accept that change will occur, and it's not always our fault. We all have an "I was wrong" or "the one that got away" story in our back pocket because of our false view of a situation. What we experience sometimes is past unhealed wounds that were triggered. We often think rejection is only given, but we, too, can project it onto others. We may assume that one action a person does is the same as one from the past. This is where a mind shift must take place. Just because it happened then, it doesn't mean it will happen again with everyone you meet. Once learned, it will be even more impactful to your life. This is something we have to be taught, especially when it comes to relationships. Remembering you are still valuable even when change occurs is important. Forgiveness is another powerful tool, so make sure you use it. You should also remember that you can't be all things to everyone. Pace yourself! Continue to practice saying "no" if it's not going to bring you joy.

Keep in mind that, in some cases, you might need the support of a professional (coach or counselor) to help you navigate past the rejection from traumatic experiences, and that's ok! That's what they were created to do.

Reflection Moment:

Take a moment now to reflect on a moment when you felt rejected, unseen, unheard, disrespected...etc. Have you forgiven yourself and the others involved? Have you truly moved passed it? If not, what actions can you take now to move past it? If you have forgiven and moved past it, write down words of praise for your actions.

✦

I have everything I need

✦

2. Awareness

Awareness: the quality or state of being aware: knowledge and understanding that something is happening or exists. (Merriam-Webster Dictionary)

But Jesus, being aware of it, said to them, "O you of little faith, why do you reason among yourselves because you [a]have brought no bread? (NKJV Mathew 6:18)

As we go through life, we have these moments where we grow to understand on a deeper level how things, people (including yourself), places, and environments operate. Armed with this information, we begin to think more before we act or speak. We make an effort to consider the good and bad before making a decision. Then, when in full growth mode, we consider if this decision will help move us forward to achieving more of the things we desire. This means that the likelihood of making mistakes that you might regret is minimized. It brings power and understanding and keeps us from falling into traps. For example, some may call these moments red flags when you're in a relationship. You might not notice or may choose to ignore bad communication, lies, manipulation, or other issues at the beginning of a relationship because you are blinded by the catch. But when you're aware of your wants, needs, and best interests, you will seek to address the matters with urgency because you are aware of the impact they will have on you. In a nutshell, when you are aware of who you are, along with your wants, needs, and environment, you have the opportunity to make better decisions. This, my friend, means that you're becoming AWARE of your value! In some cases, this process starts with small changes. Still, as Sarah Jakes Roberts says, "Your little is more than enough for you.... And it has brought you this far." So keep on going and growing!

Let's pause and reflect for a moment on the list of things that you should know about yourself:

- Identity (what makes you unique)
- How to love yourself
- What you expect from all types of relationships (partner, family, friends, workplace, etc.)
- Your values and core values
- How different environments make you feel
- Goals (short/long term)
- Vision for your life
- Be honest with yourself
- Recognize when something isn't working out and accept reality and responsibility
- Learn to like who you are
- Triggers

I have always been strong-minded, as "they" say, but it really kicked in during my 20s when I had the pleasure of landing a paid government internship in my junior year of college. This was the job that was going to launch my career. So, I understood that some things had to change because this was a major opportunity. A career job was part of why I went to college, and it was now upon me. BTW that college was the Alabama State University, 2007 graduate. Shout out to all my ASU fans, reading and HBCU students, and future students! Back to the story, that meant I couldn't do weekly partying, no more evening class schedules, and no hanging out late with friends. On the flip side, having my own money and getting my own apartment was worth cutting those things out. It took me knowing my goals and what I wanted for my life to make those decisions, such as landing the interview, getting the job, and cutting back on things that didn't align with my career. Fast forwarding in life, that same awareness helped me get through
the messy relationships with guys and prevented me from cursing out someone in the workplace or quitting on life when it got hard. Knowing who I am and owning being "a child of God" allowed me to keep my eyes focused on my vision for my life. I couldn't put a name on how I was moving until last year. Yep, after all those years, it finally came to me when I was told by my Coach, Carla, Relationship Doula, "Myrtice, you have a keen sense of awareness of what you want for your life." I lit up inside. It was like someone actually finally saw who I was. I'm not a brat, nerd, or bougie girl. I was simply aware of who I was and where I was going. I was Determined with a capital D! I'm grateful for the changes I have made. The message here is that we all have to learn to embrace our being, which is what your eyes tell you—visual eyes, spiritual eyes, common sense eyes, and street eyes. If you have the ability to possess them all, you are a true force to be reckoned with. Now go ahead and keep reading!

Reflection Moment:

A few other things I used to aid in my awareness development were accountability partners, mastermind groups, John C. Maxwell DISC Assessment (personality test), The 5 Love Languages test, reading, and my all-time favorite thing, watching documentaries. What things can you add to your life to help improve your awareness?

Abundance is my birthright

3. Faith

Faith: a firm belief in something for which there is no proof, belief or trust in someone or something. (Merriam-Webster Dictionary) Now faith is the substance of things hoped for, the evidence of things not seen. (NKJV Hebrew 11:1)

Faith is like a lens in your eyeglasses. We put them on with the expectation that we will have the ability to see where we are going. Now that we can see clearly, we will arrive at the destination we desire. When they get foggy or damaged, we either clean them or get new ones. Some of us even upgrade to contacts or get Lasik (aka my goal), and then you really really can see, lol. Either way, we continue to go after what we desire with the confidence that we have clear vision. This is how faith works. The more you depend on it, the less stressful life will be. It takes action to use both faith and fear, so choose action.

For me, it took great faith to move from my comfortable home in Alabama (AL) to a place where I had no family while going through the tremendous loss of my best friend that same year. The move was not my choice, but my job location at that time was closing, and I was given the option of moving to Georgia (GA) or Florida (FL). I chose FL since I love the ocean, but they gave me GA. I guess God did, too, lol. I packed up and was ready to go three months later. Well, the weekend I was supposed to move, a tornado hit the city I was moving to, and I also learned
that my townhouse was not ready. I was told it would be another month before it was available for me to move in. I was feeling totally devastated. But a few days later, I prayed and went anyway with my car fully packed, and my faith filled to the max. Yeah, I was scared and sad, but my inner strength wouldn't let me show it. That's when my prayer life went to a different level, my friends. I survived living out of a hotel room and my car for a month, with ugly cries, sleepless nights, homesickness, and money woes. I had to pray and have faith that where He was sending me was where I needed to be. The move, along with great faith, has worked out and has brought me many great opportunities like a new career, meeting new people, traveling more, and becoming closer to my friends. So, now I have no regrets and I truly appreciate the lessons learned and the great blessings I received during difficult times.

Reflection Moment:

Take a look back over your life and reflect on ways you had to rely on faith to get you through the hard times. What did you do? How did you feel during the process? What parts of those lessons can you incorporate into your life today?

_____
_____
_____
_____
_____
_____
_____
_____
_____
_____
_____
_____
_____
_____
_____
_____
_____
_____
_____
_____
_____
_____
_____

*God,
I'm depending
on you*

4. Patience

Patience: the capacity, habit, or fact of being patient. (Merriam-Webster Dictionary) But those who wait on the Lord Shall renew their strength; They shall mount up with wings like eagles, They shall run and not be weary, They shall walk and not faint. (NKJV Isaiah 40:31)

Being patient is one of my biggest challenges in life, and I am still working on that. One day I hope to reach God's level of patience. Until then, I will remain a microwave child, or like the "it's my money, and I want it now" commercial people, lol. Either way, I'm that girl. But on a serious note, how do you know when to act and not act in a situation? How will we know when it's time? That's the biggest question in this entire book, and I must say I don't know. I only know how it felt in my experiences, which was defeated, cornered, or pressured. There were times when I just acted because it aligned with my values; it was going to move me forward, offer flexibility, or in some cases, more $. In many instances, it worked. Sometimes it was good to act on instinct, and other times not so good. I got a half blessing when I could have gotten more if I'd waited. Looking back, I just know the more I asked for patience and really practiced it, good things happened, and better opportunities were presented.

I remember the pressure I felt to pass an exam to keep my job. I studied and took tests, yet no luck. I even passed up a trip to California to a friend's wedding just so I could study, but still no luck. The pressure was even greater because I was considered the brains of the team (aka "unofficial team lead"). I took a total of four tests in two years, and on that fourth try, I passed. Yay! I now realize that it took a full alignment between believing in myself and embracing grace and patience for me to pass that test. To help with my confidence, I used different methods of studying like setting schedules, praying specific prayers, and understanding what I missed on the prior exams. This was downright full tunnel vision mode for a few months, lol.

Patience can often offer the best views into other people as well as prevent dangers that lie ahead. For example, if you have been wondering if a friend was shady or untrustworthy, you should allow yourself time away from that person and pray and meditate for God to show you their heart and motives. Then, begin to just listen and notice how things unfold. Basically, you're allowing the answers to come to you. Once they do arrive, you have a choice to stay or move in a direction that no longer causes you to feel uncomfortable.

Don't sabotage opportunities because you don't feel ready. Make a decision to make sure your performance matches how you feel on the inside. If it's confidence, you will appreciate and accept new challenges. If it's anxiety, you might withdraw from making the necessary decision to move you forward. Don't allow the impatience or fear of the unknown to take away from who you know you are. You have worked too hard to get to where you are now!

Reflection Moment:

Take a moment to reflect on areas where more patience can be added to help reduce some of life's stressors or pressure. What areas have you been told to be patient in but are ignoring? What benefits would you gain if you were more patient?

_____
_____
_____
_____
_____
_____
_____
_____
_____
_____
_____
_____
_____
_____
_____

Situations are only temporary

5. Fear

Fear: an unpleasant, often strong emotion caused by anticipation or awareness of danger. (Merriam-Webster Dictionary)

So do not fear, for I am with you; do not be dismayed, for I am your God. I will strengthen you and help you; I will uphold you with my righteous right hand. (NKJV Isaiah 41:10)

Fear is a very expensive IT! It can rob you of mind space that could be used to help make the decisions to get you to the next level you desire. Think of the millionaires and billionaires in the tech world. You rarely see them in fancy clothes or in blogs on social issues. When you do see them, they are in plain clothes because they value using their brain to build their companies and future more than some of us do. Next, fear steals your time. You might be like me and think of every "what if" scenario, good and bad, and then still not go after the wins, opting to stay paused. That is straight, unhealthy thinking mode on 10, smh. Now you might be saying, "Ok, what do I do then?" You can start by getting back into a positive mindset mode.

Questions to ask yourself:

- Are you working too hard at this?
- Has panic set in?
- Have you become desperate?

If yes, then you are definitely in over your head, and it's time to recalibrate, just as a GPS does when we refuse to take the right turn it said we needed to take; another path might be available. Delegate what you can and try to relax, breathe, pray, and go with the flow. Release that negative energy into action steps that will help you get what you're seeking beyond the fear. On the other hand, disrespectful people will have you think otherwise. It's hard to deal with fearful people. We can't reason with them if they are in fear. I only advise that you repeat the above methods and pray for their lack of understanding.

If you have allowed yourself to stay in the workplace where you are undervalued because you feared the unknown, you are not alone. Yep, I've been there. The first time it took 13 years; yes, I said 13 years. It was cool at first because I felt that I was in my dream job (at the time), and I was on a learning curve. I loved some of the people and enjoyed the work duties, travel, and location. I even went back to school for my master's degree on tuition assistance and got other skill certifications.

After about seven years, the distractions from the things I loved, in the beginning, began to shed away, and I felt the difference in the office. I didn't feel valuable. I was assigned tasks that were mediocre for my position and felt micromanaged. There was also the pay chart that read, "You're near the end." When I asked for career advice, it was minimized to "There isn't anything (positions) right now" or "Let's discuss you working on other projects." Finally, I realized that I had to create my own path, and I decided to take another job. The opportunity came after accepting a position transfer to another office located out of state. I was fearful at times because I was on a new learning curve in a new state. But the feeling of being wanted and my value being seen outweighed all the negatives.

I must remind you that I never said that I was perfect or that I couldn't handle correction. I just understood that I was Great, aka highly favored. I know I'm great because I feel it in my soul, and God confirms it in his word, Psalms 104:1. This applies to you too! Therefore, I will not allow my fears to hold me from my future. Pressing through fears and tears is sometimes the name of the game.

Reflection Moment:

Take this time to reaffirm who you are and stand up to the fears that are running through your mind. See affirmations or repeat the I AM statements listed in the book. Next, you can look up passages in the bible to confirm you are bigger than your fears, for example, "we are more than conquerors...." Romans 8:37-39 MSG.

*I will make
an impact on my
life and others*

6. Surrender

Surrender: to yield to the power, control, or possession of another upon compulsion or demand. (Merriam-Webster Dictionary)
Trust in the LORD with all your heart and lean not on your own understanding; In all your ways acknowledge Him, And He shall direct your paths. (NKJV Proverbs 3:5–6)

Surrender is the IT that is most impactful. The action looks like you, forgiving yourself and releasing all the things that don't serve you in being your best You. There is a great release of energy and brain space when we surrender. As the song says, "this battle is not yours; it's the Lord's." Well, when does He play His role in the battle if we are doing all the work? He steps in when we surrender and goes to work to either instantly fix it, help us through it, or aid us in finding a solution.

For me, it all began when I sat down for my first counseling session. I came to the process with the realization that it was time to make all that I was going through make sense. I decided that I would surrender my brain to someone else to look inside and tell me how to organize it and function. Maybe it was the time I decided to mix up my career a little. I applied for a Rotation Program Assignment that would allow me to work in another position and branch of the organization for 3–12 months. The goal for the organization was to build more cross-training opportunities. Participants could choose from different locations around the world. When I saw California, I knew immediately that that's where I wanted to go. At the time, I had been in a relationship for five years, but it was a rocky one, and I needed this break for me and my career. I applied and was chosen for a 3-month assignment. I was super excited, but the reaction of most people around me, including my boyfriend, was the opposite. I was told that I should not go that far by myself and was asked why I was moving, as it meant leaving my relationship. I was also told that I was crazy or wrong for leaving my life for my job. Let's just say I'm glad I knew how to waterproof my mind to let all that negativity wash off and not ruin the opportunity. I sat down and made a pros/cons list to help make all that I was going through make sense. When I was finished, I surrendered all my thoughts, fears, and what-ifs to God. Yes, it was scary and risky, but I understood that on the other side of those feelings was my freedom to move forward.

Reflection Moment:

It takes faith to surrender. For me, faith is knowing that you understand that something is beyond your control and that you need help. Sometimes just breathing deep breaths or writing down your thoughts is a form of surrendering. If you struggle to decide what you need to surrender, see the list below (feel free to add more).

How about we pause now for a reflection moment?

- Understanding
- Control of others
- Future outcomes
- Rejection
- Fears
- Doubt
- Sickness
- Loneliness
- Frustrations
- Sins

_____
_____
_____
_____
_____
_____
_____
_____
_____
_____
_____
_____

Amazing and resourceful people are attached to me

7. Prayer

Prayer: an address (such as a petition) to God or a god in word or thought. (Merriam-Webster Dictionary)
Rejoice always, pray without ceasing, in everything give thanks; for this is the will of God in Christ Jesus for you. (NKJV 1 Thessalonians 5:16–18)

Prayer is the most powerful weapon a person can possess, Psalms 23. It helps enhance your beliefs and will to believe in yourself and others. When we pray, we are opening our hearts to God and allowing Him to work in us and through us, which ultimately allows us to grow more spiritually and strengthen our relationship with God. Prayer enables us to make a connection to the source that holds all our answers to the 99 questions that flow through our minds. When we pray, we sometimes get replies immediately, but other times it takes work to get an answer. Thus, we must have consistency and patience, especially when we expect answers that will help us fulfill our purpose or desires in life. Consistency means continuing to pray without ceasing. Then after you pray, believe, and take action toward what you want.

For those that are still learning to pray, I advise using scriptures or just talking to God as though you are talking to your best friend. When it comes to prayer, it's totally based on having an honest and vulnerable conversation with God. He just wants to know that you find Him trustworthy and valuable to guide your life. Yep, it is that simple.

Another way to pray is by journaling prayers, as this helps avoid the awkwardness of talking to the air, lol. It also allows you to reflect on the prayers that have previously helped you accomplish goals or overcome life's greatest challenges.

Meek Mills feat. Justin Timberlake – Believe (November 30, 2020).

Journal entry, November 30, 2020, that song touched my soul at the right point in time, as I was going through the process of finding myself again after having to be strong and playing many roles during my mom's cancer battle. Most of all, I was nurse and driver. Asking for help was hard but needed. My family medical leave assistance (FMLA) was denied by my employer during this time, so I was forced to use lots of time off from work or try and juggle work and medical appointments. I needed extra support, so I prayed not just for Mom's healing but for my own endurance, strength, and courage to get through the process and not lose myself or fall behind on duties. I made it through with the extra grace and mercy!

Lastly, prayer helps with weeding out the doubt, chaos, and confusion that occur as we journey through life. It's through that time spent in prayer that we get to know a better way to be, the way God prefers us to be, and the impact it would have on our life.

Reflection Moment:

In what ways can you improve your prayer life?

_____
_____
_____
_____
_____
_____
_____
_____
_____
_____
_____
_____
_____
_____
_____
_____
_____
_____
_____
_____

I have a mindset that can handle life changes and abundance at all levels

8. Growth

Growth: a stage in the process of growing. (Merriam-Webster Dictionary). And let us not grow weary while doing good, for in due season we shall reap if we do not lose heart. (NKJV Galatians 6:9)

Most of us automatically think of growth as a physical thing such as weight, height, hair length, and so on. Many fail to measure growth in terms of where they are now versus where they have been or where they come from. We rarely do so because it's hard to look back due to the past being filled with pain, anger, or disappointment. I, too, struggle at times with looking back. I get it. However, if you're striving for that next level and need that motivation or the willpower to get unstuck, you must get it done. When you look back, only do it for a few moments and focus on the WINS you had. Ponder on times when you were joyful and the good memories made intentionally or unintentionally. You should also reflect on the times when you were broken mentally, spiritually, or financially but still survived. Think of the sacrifices you made for yourself and others. You did it! You made the impact on you, and even if no one else acknowledged it, you and God just did!

As a child, we learned to talk first, then how to walk. Then we learned more as we journeyed through school and life. We grew! This too can be the same way by acknowledging our life, mindset, and growth. It's ok to grow. Grow beyond where you are, the environment or people. This is what God wants us to achieve, as this is His will and purpose.

We were designed to withstand, but that requires that we push ourselves beyond our boundaries or mental limitations. There was once a point in time in my life when I went hard for everything — money, men, attention, business — just in straight 24/7 work mode. Yet, this drive brought many ups and downs. Because I was the one considered smart, money savvy and had a "good job," I was often called upon to support others mentally and financially. I ended up loaning money even when I needed it. I did so because of my compassion and my expectation that the person would do the right thing and pay me back. But lies or life always happened for them, which in turn caused problems for me. Oh, how about that time in my life I wanted a guy and a relationship so badly that I was willing to do anything necessary? My boundaries were invisible, as you can see. I wasn't proud of my actions, and eventually, I realized things had to change if I wanted a different outcome.

I learned the power of saying "no," which is a full sentence when used correctly without an explanation. Some may find saying "no" mean or harsh. But it's honesty, and if you're going to set and maintain boundaries, you will have to always walk in your honest truth. Some might desire an explanation, but it is your choice whether you provide it. To learn more on this, see Nedra Glover Tawweb, Therapist and Boundaries Expert, on IG and Facebook; her gems are worth the scroll. Overall, I just want you to be ok with the growth that you see within yourself. Change is inevitable but good change will benefit you always!

Some tools to help aid in a growth mindset: use affirmations (use affirmations throughout the book), support groups, life coaching, yoga, meditation, and community service projects.

Reflection Moment:

Let's pause and reflect for a moment. In which areas of your life have you experienced growth? Where do you want to grow next? What changes do you have to make now to achieve your goal?

_____
_____
_____
_____
_____
_____
_____
_____
_____
_____
_____
_____

I enjoy being present

9. Transition

Transition: a period or phase in which such a change or shift is happening. (Merriam-Webster Dictionary)
And do not be conformed to this world, but be transformed by the renewing of your mind, that you may prove what is that good and acceptable and perfect will of God. (Romans 12:2)

When a transition begins, it can feel like a rollercoaster, which is fun to ride when you are a teen or in your 20s. But when you hit your 30s, it becomes frightening, and no part of you would dare ride. Maybe taking a long ride in your favorite sports car instead would be less frightening but also fun. So, in that statement, I shared how we change as we mature and can no longer withstand something. But to arrive at our fun place, we have to change the way we seek fun. This, too, can be applied to our goals in life. We may need to go through a transition process, which may include a combination of changes (mentally, physically, spiritually, financially, and socially), especially when you're trying to achieve a new career position or become an entrepreneur. When you have ambitious goals, you might have to move to another location and meet new people. Then you must learn more about business operations and managing financials, including what it takes to become financially stable, the power of credit, staying on budget, how to create more income, investing, marketing, writing business plans, goal setting, and so on. I aspire to be a millionaire entrepreneur one day, so I started by getting a financial manager to help with accountability and advise me on how I could become more responsible for the financial well-being of my coins and company. These past two years have been an interesting challenge, but I can see the positive impact this process has had on my money management skills and freedom to venture into some investing in myself, such as publishing this book. My message here is that it takes openness, flexibility, and dedication to blossom into the best version of YOU to achieve your IT. It will be hard at times, but it will be worth it! Leaving comfort is always hard but is necessary. At times, you have to risk becoming uncomfortable to become the unstoppable and resilient You!

All transition journeys begin with acceptance, as it is necessary to accept where you currently are in your mind before you can move on to who you are. You also need to accept that things will change for good and bad. Still, if you persevere, in the end, you will know your WHY (why you are doing what you are doing). Then it takes being obedient with the small things and the things that move you toward the finish line.

For me, it took great obedience to stay home and write this book when all I wanted was to eat some chicken wings and have a drink at the bar or simply lounge on my sofa with wine and Netflix playing all night, lol. Buuuuut, I found that providing you with the words you needed to hear to get to that next level was much more valuable.

Consistency is up next! You have to try your best to stay on track. Whether it means working every day on a task, working three long nights a week, or delegating some of your responsibilities to someone else, be like Nike and "Just Do It." Most importantly, don't be afraid to repeat something for more understanding. Keep going! Distractions will come, and you might have to increase your prayer life or get an accountability partner to stay on track, but keep going. Lastly, always be willing to take the risk and bet on yourself. God will not bring you that far to leave you! Remember, I told you this book was seven years in the making, but I did it! I just had to transition to the right place, time, and mindset. So yes, the transition process is uncomfortable and hard, but what lies on the other side, which is your next level, is sooooo worth it!

Reflection Moment:

For our reflection moment, describe a time when you made a transition that was hard. What tools did you use to keep going? Have you celebrated the wins? If you celebrated the wins from your hard work, what did you do, and how did it make you feel? If not, take this moment to plan out something to do.

_____
_____
_____
_____
_____
_____
_____
_____
_____
_____

I have divine health, wealth, love, and protection

10. Relationships

Relationship: a state of affairs existing between those having relations or dealings. (Merriam-Webster Dictionary)
In your relationships with one another, have the same mindset as Christ Jesus. (NIV Philippians 2:5)

Relationships are one constant thing we will have in life. Whether it is with family, friends, coworkers, or neighbors, we all must learn to coexist, and I hope that it will be on the best terms. In some cases, it's not always that easy because we change. We grow, or certain situations change us. Adaptation must occur in order for us to coexist through the change. At times this change may mean learning how to communicate in a way we all understand, verbally or nonverbally (i.e., through actions). Allow those around you to be who they are, and you stay true to who you are. Depending on how valuable the relationship is to you, you must be willing to do the work. Devotion is required to build the kind of relationship you're seeking. This is where we have to rely on faith and prayer. If the relationship is organic, it will sustain the ups and downs, and you will value it dearly. On the other hand, if the relationship does not work out the way you desire, find a way to be ok with that. You gave it your best! God saw you and will reward your efforts by granting you someone even better.

Just know that in all your different relationships, you need to work on communication, which means expressing all your wants and needs. For example, my communication style is very direct. In my relationships, I ask others to speak to me as directly as possible. Yes, give me all the details! This way, I minimize the need for clarification or gray areas. Still, I am aware that not everyone can handle my direct approach, so I have to find ways to communicate with them on their level. In some situations, this requires more texting and emails and less direct talking, while other cases involve face-to-face conversations so they could read my behavioral gestures. Either way, the goal is to find a balance in the way you communicate so you can thrive in your relationships. Remember to be true to yourself and voice what makes you who you are!

Lastly, when building or redefining a relationship, consider the circle method. You have 10 lines that form a circle with the outermost people being valuable to your life but don't impact it on a daily basis. Then you have your middle, the reliable ones, and last, the core. The core should only be the people who know you best. These individuals have helped you battle the good and bad, ugly, happy, and sad moments. They offer honesty and unbiased opinions, and you find them most valuable and trust that they can help drive you forward. The core people are also the ones with whom you are your most vulnerable and most authentic self. If at any time you feel that a certain relationship's value has decreased, go back to your circle to see how that individual affects your life. If needed, get the help you need to keep going if you're in a stuck moment.

Remember, not everyone has to know everything about you to love, like, and support you. So, I advise that you share and give your time wisely to those in your circle. The circle also helps you reflect on who has your best interests when times become lonely. You can look back and see you're not alone.

In relationships, blending lives is hard and takes work. But just make sure you know that our happiness is not dependent on someone else doing or saying something for you. You are responsible for maintaining that in your life.

Reflection Moment:

Pause now and reflect on building a relationship circle. Ask yourself these questions: Who is included? What impact do they have on my life?

_____
_____
_____
_____
_____
_____
_____
_____
_____

The me
I see
is
enough for me

11. Love

Love: a strong affection for another arising out of kinship or personal ties. (Merriam-Webster Dictionary)
Love bears all things, believes all things, hopes all things, endures all things. (NKJV 1 Corinthians 13:7)

Love is a tool that will keep you going no matter what the situation may be. Love can bring us some of the worst pain, but it will also bring us the most joyous moments of our life. It is the most beautiful thing you see expressed by people, and you are blessed if you feel it and give it. There are various types of love, including Agape (selfless), Storge (unconditional), Eros (romantic), and Philia (Friendship). I only learned this when I hit my 30s, smh. Before then, I thought that love was love, lol. But over the course of my life, I have had the pleasure of experiencing love in many of its forms. To me, it's the one value I was taught as a child growing up, mostly in church. "Thou shalt love the Lord thy God with all thy heart, and with all thy soul, and with all thy mind." This is the first and greatest commandment. "And the second is like unto it, Thou shalt love thy neighbor as thyself" (Matthew 22:37–39). Because of this and the rejection I experienced, I have loved hard in all my relationships. On this journey, I have learned to set boundaries with love too. Even though I gave it 100%, it hasn't always been gifted to me in the way I wanted or needed. I often found this painful, but I still gave love unconditionally. One of my experiences with unreciprocated love involves my father. Still, despite having an estranged relationship for years, when he was stricken with heart problems, I set aside my issues to go and see him. I visited him multiple times, and he appreciated me for coming. I felt a genuine love from him, but had it not been for me consistently allowing myself to love unconditionally and heal through my hurts, I probably wouldn't have done it. When you love, it hurts when it's taken away. This especially occurs when people you love are no longer in your life due to death. But if I never loved them, I wouldn't be able to reminisce on the joyful times I shared with them, which allowed me to move forward.

My challenge to you is to be open to love. Analyze and experiment with the types of love I listed above. Never shut yourself off from experiencing one of God's great blessings. If you have been severely damaged by love, be sure to get some form of support or accountability from a therapist, coach, or trusted friend. This will help you not to fall back into the same guilty feelings. The recovery process from loving and losing love is something we have to work through in life. This may mean being vulnerable to strangers at times. It also means reintroducing yourself to others, especially if you're single. Whatever you do, don't shut down!

Acceptance is always the key. Love doesn't have to always come from family. Others in our lives are able to provide it too. Some of my greatest love moments have come from those outside my family. The value that's been added to my life from their compassion is unmeasurable. You should also keep in mind that some people just don't have the capacity to say what you need to hear or show you the love and appreciation you desire. It's sad to know, but we have to be ok with that because, at the end of the day, God does appreciate it and will bless you along the way. Replace poison with love!

Reflection Moment:

List the things you love about yourself. Then ask how you can improve the love you give to others.

_____
_____
_____
_____
_____
_____
_____
_____
_____
_____
_____
_____
_____
_____
_____
_____

I did my best today, and that is enough

12. Believe

Believe: consider to be true or honest. (Merriam-Webster Dictionary)
I can do all things through Christ who strengthens me. (Philippians 4:13)

I believe in you! I believe in you! And one more time for the people in the back, lol; I believe in you!

When you believe, you have a roadmap to who you want to become, and it all starts with you! To be honest, I really didn't see the fullness of my life until I started believing in myself. Between the ages of 23 to 25, you couldn't tell me I wasn't the baddest *****, as the rapper Trina says, lol. I believed I could do it all at that time, including running a relationship, a hair store business, and a career. Then, when things took a dive, I was left holding the bag, well, an empty bag, lol. I felt tired, doubtful, defeated, unloved, unseen, etc. I just existed. I had no passion for anything. I knew something had to change because I didn't like the ME I was living with. That's when I took the leap of faith and hired a life/business coach, Tasha M. Scott. I had to learn to believe in myself again. Slowly, as the journey progressed, I could see the ME I wanted to be. She saw me and guided me on how to discover my next level. The icing on the cake was my learning how to incorporate God into everything—life, daily routines, relationships, business, and career. This wasn't an easy ride. It took being vulnerable, making financial investments in myself, giving a full commitment, and being prayerful to survive the journey. Only you know what lies inside of you! This is what lights you up and what keeps you going, so it will always be worth it.

In the Bible story of David, he did not build the temple but made the plans and passed them on to his son Solomon (1 Chronicles 6-8). Either way, it doesn't matter who carried the plans out, the belief was set, and the purpose was achieved. Ultimately, you need to learn to know God for yourself! The more you believe, the more the roadmap to how it can be achieved will be developed. See the scripture Psalms 32:8 to instruct you. Go make your plans and a vision board and start believing! Remember, don't ever quit God because he won't quit on you!

Reflection Moment:

Read this quote by the honorable Michelle Obama below. Write out how you feel when you read it. What story lies inside of you? How valuable are your stories to you?

> "You have to believe your story has value" - Michele Obama

Lack does not exist in my life

13. Boundaries

Boundaries: a line that marks the limits of an area; a dividing line. (Merriam-Webster Dictionary)
Prepare yourself and be ready, you and all your companies that are gathered about you, and be a guard for them. (NKJV Ezekiel 38:7)

Once you have unlocked the value of who you are and where you're going, you have to learn to honor and protect your mind, environment, health, etc. This is where the boundaries come into play. Everyone's boundaries look different, but most include maintaining a level of respect for your life in the areas of physical, sexual, emotional, spiritual, time, financial, and valued possessions. This also includes items that are non-negotiable, "aka you ain't changing it." You know how uncomfortable it makes you feel when someone crosses you wrong, Right? You just want to curse at them, scream, yell, and sometimes cry because it's just that sad or embarrassing. That is why you need your boundaries to avoid such behaviors from affecting your focus and positive energy. A few examples include when your friend is late all the time, but you have reservations, or when someone chooses to talk about a situation that you asked them not to, especially in public, or you explained something to a coworker, but they consistently ignore the instructions so you will do the work. Now the one we all can relate to is the gossiping friend, as we all know a person that always has something to say about others' lives, and it is usually not good. These examples are all things that affect you often and can make you lose focus, and, at times, bring negativity into your life. If it begins to bother you when it occurs, then a boundary needs to be established. I have asked people not to talk about others around me, and I would change the subject every time they do or ask them not to include me in their gossiping conversations. Rethink the boundaries set up around your life. Are you trying to live up to your own expectations or someone else's?

Taking one's own advice is often the hardest thing to do, but it is necessary. Trust me; I've been there. Try trusting yourself for once; you're worth the fight!

Since leaving home for college at age 18, I have always been the one who traveled home for family and friends' events. If there was a gathering, I was there no matter the cost (health, time, or money). I loved my family and making memories with them. However, over time, that cost took a toll on me mentally, physically, and financially. I also lost a relationship over it. Yep, I repped the "family first" motto hard. But once I took a deep dive into how I was feeling, I became well aware of the cost.

I was failing to give myself the opportunity to learn my new environment and save $ for things I really wanted or rest. Unfortunately, I was comfortable being uncomfortable at that time. Later, I wanted a different outcome and to feel good in my decision-making, rather than feeling guilty or as if I was being used. I also wanted to be relaxed more and not always on the go. So I started weighing the cost of the invites to attend events and setting boundaries. In some instances, I contributed financially, while others received my time only. Lastly, I chose the option to opt-out completely. Yes, it hurt to tell family no at first because all the what ifs would flow through my mind. But after I began to see the rewards I was providing for myself it felt ok. The moral of the story is that it is ok to say "no" to them and "yes" to you! Listen to you sometimes. You matter just as much as them. I allowed myself to do that, and you can too!

Reflection Moment:

At this moment of reflection, consider these things for maintaining your boundaries:

- Control who is allowed in your space, both personally and professionally
- Will yourself to be peaceful
- Value your time
- Become extra loving to yourself by practicing self-love on a daily basis
- Ask yourself often, "How comfortable am I with myself?"
- Be open to expressing your expectations and level of tolerance to other people
- Stay away from blaming thoughts
- Take personal responsibility for addressing the problems you have
- Ask more questions and listen closely to the answers before responding
- Listen more than speaking
- Maintain an energy budget
- Remember people pleasing isn't love; it is fear
- Only justify your choices when you feel it is necessary
- Always stay honest with yourself

All you need to do is push beyond the boundaries set by your doubts or others. What other boundaries do you need to set?

I release control to try and control another

14. Freedom

Freedom: the quality or state of being exempt or released, usually from something onerous. (Merriam-Webster Dictionary)
And you shall know the truth, and the truth shall make you free. (NKJV John 8:32)

We have finally made it to the last IT, yay! I'm proud of you for making it this far. Freedom is the ultimate goal, and it is attained when we know our truth. The more growth work we achieve, the more freedom we allow into our mind, body, and spirit.

I personally feel like I haven't fully arrived at this point, but I'm extremely close. I have had freedom moments that I have celebrated. But I have committed myself to stay on the course until I arrive at full freedom. Some might ask, "Well, how do you know when you have achieved it?" I don't know. This is something only you will know when you have achieved your freedom. Some may use vision boards or a checklist to track their progress, while others would rely on feelings based on a deep reflection. Perhaps the answer will come from God through prayer. However, you choose to receive the answer is ok as long as you remember that the goal is to value your thoughts and opinions more than those of others. God gave us gut intuition (aka discernment) for a reason, and we must use it. His word is our truth to stand on, and it's 100% reliable. Stand on it and make the decisions that you know are aligned with His word, and you will move forward. If He leads you to a path where people walk away, opportunities are limited, things are difficult or abnormal, etc., just know it's worth the journey because He is leading you.

(Proverbs 3:5-6)
It is my sincere hope as we come to a close that you are able to feel a few chains (stress, pressure, negativity) loosening from your life. You are ok! Your IT has a title now! You are doing the work, and it shall pay off; YAY!

Reflection Moment:

Now here is your last reflection moment: Begin to ask yourself what your freedom looks like. How does it make you feel? List how you track when you have arrived at your freedom moments.

Be sure to check out the resources below to help you with the journey. Be Brave, Be blessed!

*With God,
I can do all things*

Resources

Characters in Bible for Empowerment
Mary
David
Mark
Isaiah
Esther
Eve
Ruth
Naomi
Woman with issue of blood
Paul
Woman at the well

Helpful Books and Influencers
Woman Evolve - Sarah Jakes Roberts
Becoming - Michelle Obama
Leadershift – John C. Maxwell
Mind Right, Life Right – Ash Cash
She's Still There – Chrystal Evans Hurst
Will – Will Smith
Let Love Have the Last Word – Common
Hustle Harder, Hustle Smarter – Curtis 50 Cent Jackson
The Richest Man in Babylon – George Clason & Mitch Horowitz
QBQ! The Question Behind the Question – John G. Miller
Eat, Pray Love – Elizabeth Gilbert
The Truths We Hold – Kamala Harris
The Go Giver – Bob Burg & John David Mann
Soar – T.D. Jakes
Set Boundaries, Find Peace – Nedra Glover Tawwab
Unf—k Your Brain – Faith G. Harper

"I Am" Statements

- I am strong, determined, valued, loved, courageous, and secure
- I am highly favored
- I am full of grace and mercy
- I am creative
- I am full of purpose
- I am enough
- I am brave, beautiful, and bold
- I am what the world needs
- I am who God wants me to be
- I am right where I need to be
- I am everything I want to be
- I am a generational curse breaker
- I am healed from overthinking
- I am healed from regrets, past pain and trauma, rejection, and fears

Acknowledgments

To my friends and family, you know who you are; thanks for allowing me the space and opportunity to produce this book! Your support has been like good music to my ears. Big thanks to my Mom for always showing me what bravery looks like, and I appreciate it! Lastly, to my Angels (Grandma Bay, Auntie Deb, and my friends Gomez, Mike & Sabrina), the support given while on earth and now in heaven has been unwavering and helped push me through this process; thank you!

About Me

It has taken years of counseling, life coaching, leadership, and education to help improve my life so I can be the best version you see of me today. I'm the career girl, friend girl, life of the party girl, supporter, daughter, auntie, mentor, coach, manager, director ... you name it, I have a shirt for it, lol. Though it brought a lot of attention, I still found myself in rooms full of people, yet I still felt lonely or like I was missing something. I then began to try and figure out what I needed to do. I tried diving into education. I got a master's degree and then started dating, hoping that having a partner would fill the hole. Next, there was drinking, partying, and traveling, but still no luck. I then decided to tap into my entrepreneurial side by opening a business (beauty supply store). I was in full hustle mode with too much work and barely any play. Then burnout occurred, and I thought maybe just focusing on one thing would be the key, so I chose work and career growth. That was a blessing and a curse because I realized I was micromanaged, undervalued, and stuck in a position with no growth potential. Anxiety kicked in, and I was in total " what would Jesus do (WWJD) mode" because I didn't have any idea what to do with my life. Everyone around me said I was great, but they did not realize that I was drowning in what-ifs, anger, relationship drama, loneliness, and identity issues, and my confidence was straight gone. I lacked the focus to make the next move. Finally, after tons of silent cries and prayers, I was introduced to life coaching and counseling, which helped tremendously. Ultimately, I have learned to allow THEM (all the negativity of people, thoughts, places, and things) to have their way but not get distracted.

Still, one of the most impactful things that helped me was reading more to increase my spiritual knowledge. I learned what God's word had to say about me. It lit me up just as one of my favorite Lil Wayne or Chris Brown songs would if I were at a party. He let me know I was beautiful, with a dash of fearful and wonderfully made (Psalms 139:14). Finally, I was reassured that I wasn't alone! Thereafter, I started a journey to truly living a limitless life. My energy tolerance budget is now hella bougie!

www.ingramcontent.com/pod-product-compliance
Lightning Source LLC
Chambersburg PA
CBHW051603010526
44118CB00023B/2804